The Pied Piper

Retold by Adèle Geras
Series Advisor Professor Kimberley Reynolds
Illustrated by Ian Beck

OXFORD
UNIVERSITY PRESS

Letter from the Author

I went to boarding school by the sea in Brighton and I loved it there. I haven't any brothers or sisters so all these ready-made friends were a real treat. After school, I studied French and Spanish at Oxford University and I've been writing books for children for forty years.

I like retelling well-known stories because it's great to try and make something new and a bit different out of a tale that's already been told. *The Pied Piper* is a favourite of mine because those rats are YUCK and the whole thing is a bit creepy ... I love Robert Browning's poem too, called *The Pied Piper of Hamelin*.

Adèle Geras

Nobody knew where they'd come from, but one day the rats were there. Some people said they lived in the mud along the banks of the river Weser, which ran through the town of Hamelin. Others thought they had come from the forests which grew on the hills nearby.

The rats were everywhere. They ran down alleyways and up drainpipes. They scampered over floors, tap-tapping on the wood with their black claws. They trailed their pink, rubbery tails through the food in every larder. They gathered under beds and went to sleep between the sheets in the chests of drawers. They climbed into cots where babies lay dreaming. By candlelight, their eyes were like red points of fire in the darkness.

The people of Hamelin were happy and busy before the rats came to the town. The baker baked bread and cakes. The butcher's meat pies were famous for their flavour. The grocer made the tastiest pickles for miles around. Everyone was polite and smiling and said 'Good morning' to their neighbours as they passed them in the street.

But now, the people of Hamelin were in despair.

'It's a disaster!' they cried. 'Those rats are bigger than cats. Someone should do something.'

The mayor called a meeting. 'These rats,' he said, 'are a plague on our town. Can no one trap them or poison them?'

'We've tried,' said one man, 'but there are always more rats.'

'Fatter rats,' said a woman.

'Rats with sharper teeth,' added an old man.

Then a voice spoke from the back of the room. 'I will do it.'

Everyone turned to see who had spoken.

A man stood just inside the door. In one hand he held a silver flute and his clothes were half red and half yellow. He spoke again. 'I can rid Hamelin of its rats, but my price is a thousand gold coins.'

'Thank you, kind sir,' said the mayor, and everyone clapped. 'A thousand gold coins will be yours, if you really can do what you've promised.'

The man nodded and left the room. Everyone followed him out to the main street and watched to see what would happen next.

The man put the flute to his lips and began to play as he walked away down the street. Then, from every house the rats came running. A river of rats raced to follow the Pied Piper's silvery tune.

They filled the road from pavement to pavement in a moving carpet of black and brown and pale grey fur. And when the piper reached the Weser, the rats plunged down the bank and into the river. The icy water closed over their furry heads. Every one of them was drowned.

When the townspeople looked for the Pied Piper, they couldn't find him.

As the days went by, they wondered what had become of him. After a few weeks, everyone had forgotten all about the rats.

Then one day, the Pied Piper returned to Hamelin. He walked into a meeting at the Town Hall. The mayor said, 'Greetings, friend. We wondered where you were.'

'I have come to collect the thousand gold coins you promised me.'

The mayor laughed. 'A thousand coins? My dear fellow! A hundred, surely? It's ridiculous to expect a thousand gold coins for one piece of work.'

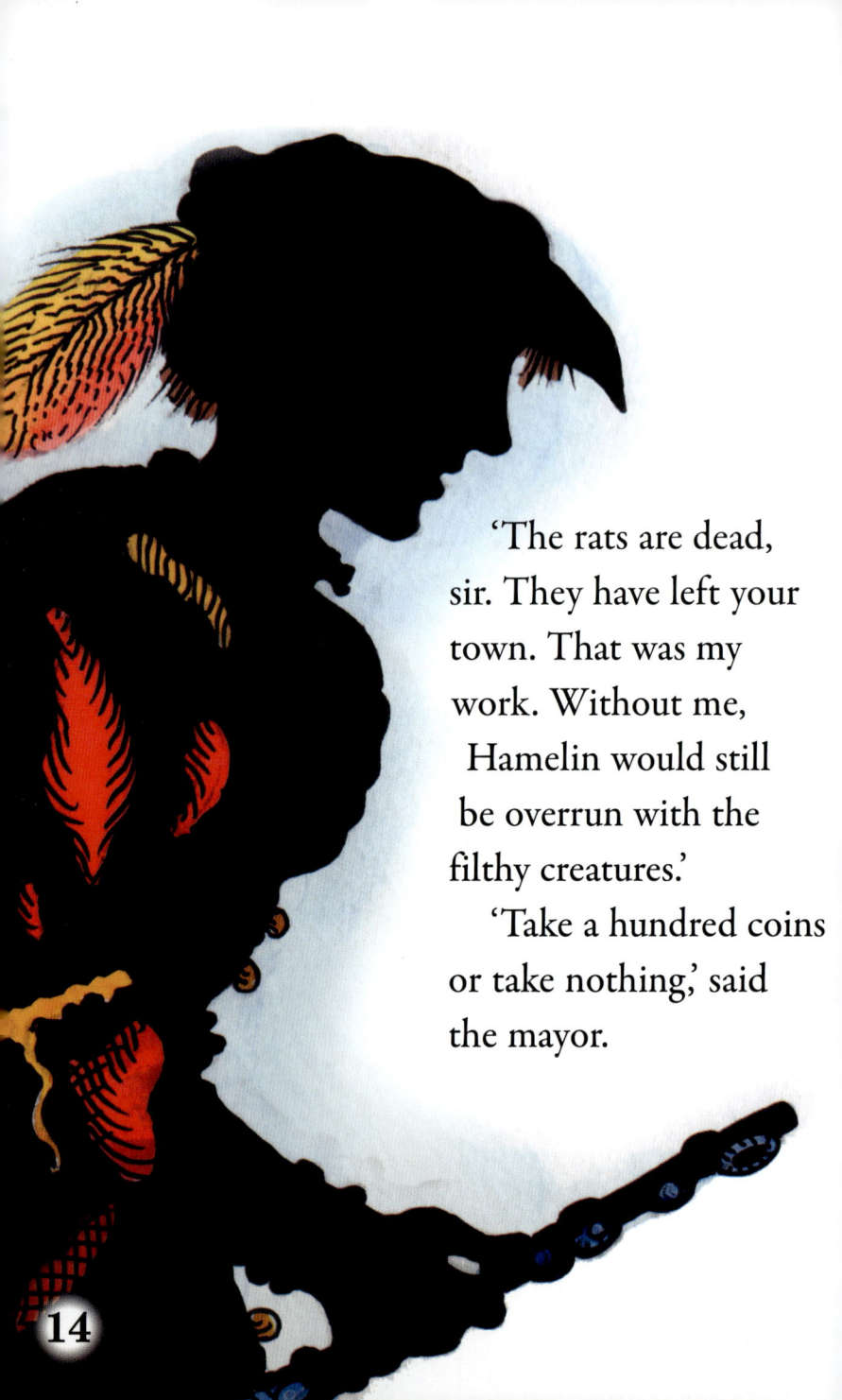

'The rats are dead, sir. They have left your town. That was my work. Without me, Hamelin would still be overrun with the filthy creatures.'

'Take a hundred coins or take nothing,' said the mayor.

The Pied Piper said, 'If you do not pay me what you promised, I will take something worth more to you than money.'

The Mayor laughed. 'Do your worst, Piper!' he said. 'We have no rats. We have a good life here in Hamelin. Leave now, and don't bother us again. Take the money we're offering and stop this nonsense about a thousand coins.'

The Pied Piper left the room. The mayor felt pleased with himself. He had saved the town a great deal of money.

For a few days, life in Hamelin continued pleasantly enough. The men and women of the town went about their business. The mayor strutted around the main square, smiling and bowing when people thanked him for ridding the town of rats.

Summer had come to the world and the river glittered in the sunlight. The children of Hamelin were happy in the open air, playing games: running, skipping, kicking a ball across the grass, and making dens along the riverbank. Everyone had forgotten about the Pied Piper.

Then one day, the Pied Piper appeared in the town again. On market day, he was sitting on the edge of the fountain in the main square. The mayor was taking his morning walk, and saw him.

'You again!' the mayor said, marching up to the young man in the strange clothes. 'I thought we'd seen the last of you.'

The Pied Piper stood up, took off his red and yellow hat, and bowed to the mayor. 'I am waiting for my thousand gold coins,' he said.

'Wait as long as you like,' said the mayor. 'You won't be getting any more gold coins from this town, I promise you.'

The Pied Piper put his hat on again.

'As you wish,' he said. He turned his back on the mayor and began to walk across the square, making his way out of the town.

The Pied Piper turned into a dark alley, and then he took out his flute and began to play. The tune was a simple melody, as sweet and golden as melted sugar. It twisted into the air and spread out into every corner of the town.

Every man and woman in Hamelin stood quite still, as though they'd been bewitched. But the children ... oh! The children were pulled towards it as if by a magnet. They had to follow, had to leave everything they had ever known, and follow the Pied Piper on and on.

The Pied Piper led the children through the streets of Hamelin, and out past the last house, and over the furthest field, and through the wood at the edge of the town.

All the children of Hamelin followed the Pied Piper through the wood to the foot of a dark mountain. They forgot everything: their parents and teachers, their homes and their beds, their toys and games, and everyone and everything they loved.

But one child could not go with them. John, on his crutches, was too slow to keep up with his friends. When the townspeople came looking for their children, John was there at the side of the road, crying.

'Where are the children?' the mayor cried. A crowd of parents was there too, weeping for their sons and daughters. 'What has become of them?'

'The Pied Piper has taken them into the mountain,' said John. 'I tried to follow, but before I got there, they had gone.'

'How can that be?' said one woman. 'They must be on the mountain.'

'No,' said John. 'A hole opened up like a huge door in the side of the mountain and they all went in, following the Pied Piper.'

'And then? What happened then?'

Everyone stood in silence as John started to cry.

'The gap in the side of the mountain closed up. They are there now, inside the mountain. Locked there forever,' said John. He burst into tears and everyone wept with him.

The Pied Piper was never seen in Hamelin ever again.